TEACH YOUR CHILD
TO
SWIM

Susan Meredith
with
Carol Hicks
Chief swimming instructor and Amateur Swimming Association staff tutor,
Crystal Palace National Sports Centre, London, United Kingdom
and
Jackie Stephens
Amateur Swimming Association tutor, Crystal Palace National Sports Centre,
London, United Kingdom

Designed by Mary Cartwright
Illustrated by Roger Fereday and Shelagh McNicholas
Photographs by Russell Cheyne (All-Sport UK) and John Bellenis
Edited by Robyn Gee

CONTENTS

With advice from:
Jean Findlay, Amateur Swimming Association tutor
Jean Cook, Amateur Swimming Association advanced teacher
Lorna Hunt, Amateur Swimming Association teacher

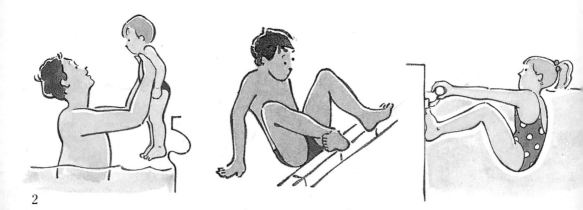

ABOUT TEACHING YOUR CHILD TO SWIM

Swimming is a very valuable skill to teach children: it increases their safety, gives them enjoyment and helps to keep them fit

Research has shown that children make most progress in swimming if they are introduced to the water by a parent. The close one-to-one relationship makes it easier to build confidence: this is essential for learning to swim. You don't have to be an expert swimmer, or even to swim at all, to get your child started, provided you are confident walking in shallow water. All you should be aiming to do in the early stages is to get your child to enjoy the water.

This book will give you plenty of ideas for safe and gentle introductory activities. The emphasis throughout is on allowing children to proceed at their own pace without being pressured.

Once your child is afloat, you will be able to move on to the sections of the book dealing with the strokes and other water skills. You may be able to use these to improve your own swimming as well as your child's or, as your child gets older, work together to improve each other's performance. In the later sections of the book the swimmer is sometimes addressed directly rather than the parent. Do encourage older children to read the book themselves and especially to look at the explanatory illustrations.

As your child makes progress, always remember that swimming should continue to be fun. Although the different strokes and skills are explained in some detail, don't become over-concerned with achieving the perfect style. Many of the best swimmers swim at least partly by instinct and would not be able to analyze what they do. Improvement often comes naturally with plenty of practice and, above all, continued enjoyment of the water.

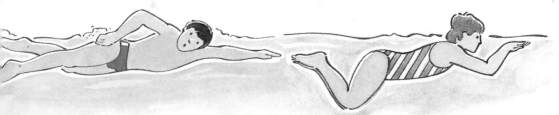

PREPARING FOR SWIMMING

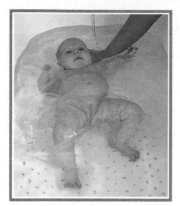

Get your baby used to going in the big bath at home before you take her to the pool.

The first step towards learning to swim is feeling at ease in the water and it is well worth planning ahead to ensure that your child's first experience of swimming is a happy one.

When to start?

Some people believe that after nine months in a fluid environment babies are born without fear of water and able to swim, so that the sooner you introduce them to the water, the better. Babies naturally move their arms and legs about when they are put in water shortly after birth and there are specific methods for teaching very small babies to learn to swim by which some spectacular results have been achieved.

However, on health grounds, it is not advisable to start going swimming too early. Besides the risk of chilling, young babies have very little natural immunity to disease. They should not be taken to a public swimming pool until three weeks after their first immunization. The three weeks give the vaccine time to be absorbed into the body. Psychologically, it is best if a baby is used to going in the big bath at home before being taken to the pool.

4 to 5 months old can be an ideal age to start swimming.

The ideal age

For many babies four to five months can be the ideal age to start going to the pool. By about six months they are usually starting to sit up and will try to do this in the water as well as out of it. By eight to nine months they are often becoming more fearful both of water and strange environments. In general, the older a child is when she first starts going swimming, the more apprehensive she is likely to be. However, there is no point in going swimming early if you do not feel that you are both ready for it.

Little and often

Once you do start, try to go swimming regularly. Your child will learn much more in short frequent visits than in the occasional long one. In any case, babies and young children should not stay in the water for long at any one time.

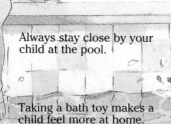

Always stay close by your child at the pool.

Taking a bath toy makes a child feel more at home.

Armbands allow a little independence.

Gentle slope.

Finding a suitable swimming pool

Swimming pool facilities vary considerably and it may be worth your while travelling a little further afield than you otherwise would to find one which has especially good facilities for babies and young children. Check on the following:

- Is there a separate pool for small children? These are often called teaching or training pools and are usually about 1m (3ft) deep throughout or graduated from ½m (1ft 6in) to 1m (3ft). It is almost essential to go in a training pool to find warm enough water and to avoid the rough-and-tumble of the main pool.

Make sure the facilities are suitable for babies and young children.

- What temperature is the water? Warm water is needed for all non-swimmers. For babies in particular it is essential, as their body heating mechanisms are not very efficient. They lose heat quickly, but do not have a shiver reflex and so can get extremely cold very quickly, with no apparent symptoms until they start turning blue. For babies and toddlers the water temperature needs to be at least 29°C (84°F) to be safe, and is better between 30°C (86°F) and 31°C (88°F). By the time a child is three, 28°C (82°F) is adequate. The air temperature should be one or two degrees above the water temperature.

Always walk through footbath.

- Are the changing facilities suitable for babies and young children? There should be changing mats or changing tables, bins for diapers, playpens to put the baby in while you get changed, and non-slip mats on the floor. The toilets should be fairly near the pool, especially for newly potty-trained toddlers.

- How deep is the shallow water? It is an advantage if there is an area of very shallow water where a child can sit, crawl or splash about.

- How do you get into the pool? Some small children would rather walk into the water than be carried. A gentle slope or wide, shallow steps are best.

- When is the pool quietest? Babies and young children are likely to be upset or distracted by a lot of noise and activity.

Keep down to child's level.

Equipment

Clothes for a baby

Babies should wear close-fitting pants or trunks in the water. They have to wear something in case they pass a stool. (Urine is made sterile by the chlorine.) On the other hand, they cannot wear a diaper or plastic pants because these would get waterlogged and make them sink.

A towel with a hood can be useful for keeping the baby's head warm after swimming.

Toys

Taking a child's favorite bath toys to the pool will help to make him feel more at home, besides being useful for specific activities in the water.

Armbands These can be useful for safety, for making a child feel at ease and for allowing some freedom of movement. Their size makes them restricting for babies under about a year and some children do not like them.

The biggest disadvantage is that children can quickly become reliant on them and be reluctant to take them off. For this reason, some experts advise against using them altogether. It is certainly wise to wait and see how a child gets on before deciding whether to use them or not.

The best type to buy are inflatable ones with double chambers and safety valves. If one chamber gets punctured, the baby will still keep afloat and you can gradually reduce the amount of air in them as the child progresses. Make sure they are small enough to stay on: they should be worn above the elbows.

Rubber rings These are not a good idea. Babies and young children can fall out of them and if they are worn with armbands they restrict movement and raise the body so high that all sense of buoyancy is lost.

Aqua-packs These are inflatable packs which strap to the back. The pressure of water can force the pack up round the neck and they tend to make the child swim vertically.

Floats Polystyrene floats are useful for encouraging horizontal movement in the water and you may be able to start using them from as early as a year old.

Goggles Babies and young children do not stay in the water long enough to need goggles. In any case, these are not made small enough to fit this age group properly and can be dangerous if the child tries to pull them off and they bounce back in her eyes.

First visit to a swimming pool

The first time you take your child to a swimming pool, it is a good idea just to look around and watch from the viewing gallery. This will give her a chance to get used to the strange atmosphere of the pool which can be very intimidating.

On your second visit you may want to get changed and go to the poolside but don't get in the water unless your child seems keen to. Don't worry if you have to repeat this a few times.

When not to go swimming

It is unwise to take babies or young children swimming if they seem even slightly unwell. They should not swim if they have a cold, or any nose, throat, chest, ear or eye infection; if they have diarrhea or any type of stomach upset; or if they have athlete's foot, which is highly contagious. Some, but not all, pools allow people with warts to swim if these are covered with a special plaster or sock. If your child has eczema, asthma or epilepsy, it is best to talk to your doctor or health visitor before going swimming.

Non-swimming parents

It is not strictly necessary for a parent to be able to swim to take a baby or young child swimming. You will be in shallow water and your child will not be ready to be taught proper strokes for some time.

However, it is vital that you do not appear nervous of the water or this will quickly be communicated to your child. If you are nervous, try to go with another adult who is confident. It may be a good idea for you to join a baby and parent class.

Baby and parent classes

These are usually for babies up to the age of about three and their parents and are an excellent way of getting you started with teaching your child to swim and encouraging you to go to the pool regularly.

Before you enrol, go and visit a class* to check on the pool's facilities, make sure the teacher has a recognized qualification** and find out if the atmosphere is happy and relaxed. The atmosphere will be quieter and the water smoother if the class has exclusive use of the pool, not of just one area roped off from other swimmers.

The class should be small enough, say ten babies each with a parent, to allow the teacher to give individual advice.

Give your child plenty of time to get used to the pool.

If you are not very confident, try to go with another adult.

Organized classes can be an excellent introduction to swimming.

7

*Find out what classes are available from the pools, the library or the local council.
** In America this will be from the American Red Cross, the American Alliance for Health, Physical Education, Recreation and Dance (AAHPERD) or YMCA.

BATH PLAY

Try to make bathtime as relaxed and happy as possible.

Sharing a bath can be fun provided you supervise closely.

Encourage him to play with toys.

One of the best ways to prepare babies and children for going swimming is to encourage them to play in the bath at home. This can help them to develop water confidence and can be especially useful for getting them used to water on their head and face.

The most practical time for bath play is at the child's usual bathtime, before you wash her, as soapy water may make her slippery to hold. Remember that bathtime is a child's first experience of water and try to keep it as relaxed and happy as possible, making sure she is not put off by feeling cold. Many babies and young children dislike having baths at some stage and none of the activities described on the next few pages should ever be forced on a child who is not showing signs of enjoyment. If a child who was previously happy in the water suddenly becomes unhappy, just revert to earlier, more gentle activities until the phase passes.

Water and air temperature

For young babies the temperature of the water needs to be between 29°C (84°F) and 32°C (90°F). The water should feel warm to your elbow or the inside of your wrist. If you want to measure the temperature really accurately, you could buy a thermometer from a hardware shop. The bathroom needs to be warm too, with the temperature as high as 24°C (75°F) if you can manage it. Very young babies should stay in the water for only about five minutes to start with. You can build this up gradually to 10-15 minutes by the age of three months.

Safety

You will need to supervise bath play very closely to prevent accidents. Never leave a baby or young child alone in the bath, even for a moment. They can drown in only small amounts of water in a very short time. This is one reason it is not a good idea to put a young baby's face right into the water, though some people may recommend it.

A non-slip bathmat provides added security.

Encourage leg kicking.

Always support baby securely.

In the baby bath

Babies are used to moving their arms and legs about in a fluid environment before birth and will do the same when they are put in water soon after birth.

If a baby is happy in the bath, try supporting her with one hand under her head and the other under her bottom and move her gently backwards and forwards. Don't let water splash in her face.

It is worth trying to get a baby used to water on his head and face right from the start. Gently squeeze a sponge over the back of his head and, if he enjoys it, let a little water trickle over his face.

The next step is to use containers to pour water over the baby's head, back and shoulders. Again, you can let a small amount of water go over his face so long as he does not object.

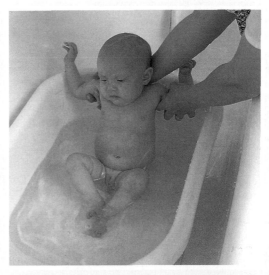

Some babies are ready to go into the big bath at two or three months old. A good intermediate step is to put the baby bath inside the big bath so the baby can get used to the larger area gradually.

9

In the big bath

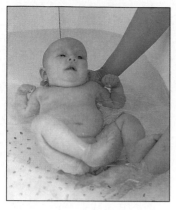

When the baby is at home in the bath, you can start getting her used to the feeling of water supporting her body by repeating the gentle backwards and forwards movement suggested on page 9 for the baby bath.

A baby under about six months may float happily on her back with just a hand under her head.

The baby may also like lying on her front. Support her under her arms and move her gently backwards and forwards For a young baby who still cannot support her head, you will need to stretch your fingers out under her chin to prevent her face going in the water. Don't insist on putting her on her front if she dislikes it.

Once the baby can sit up, give her things to play with. Containers are good because they may encourage her to pour water over herself. Besides proper bath toys, try plastic containers from the kitchen and spoons, a ladle, strainer and funnel. If you intend to use armbands at the pool, let her play with these too.

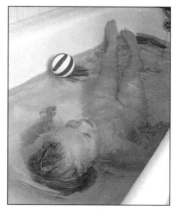

Encourage the baby to splash with his hands by putting toys in front of him and showing him how to push them along. It is better to let him do the splashing although he may enjoy being gently splashed on the lower half of his body.

Encourage an older baby or child to lie flat with her shoulders or, even better, her ears under the water at each bathtime. Afterwards, let the water drain from her ears by tilting her head first to one side for a few seconds, then the other. Then dry with a towel.

An older baby or young child may enjoy walking her hands or forearms along the bottom of the bath while kicking her legs gently. She can do this on her back as well as on her front.

Having a bath together

This can be great fun for both parent and child, from the age of about two months, and does a lot to build confidence, especially if a child is nervous of water. It is easier if a second person is there to lift the baby in and out of the bath and to dry him. A shared bathtime is also an excellent opportunity for blowing bubbles (see right).

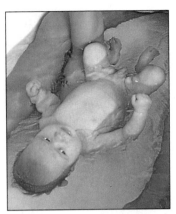

As you sit in the bath, let the baby lie in your lap, on either her back or front, and move her legs to simulate kicking. It is worth repeating the word "kick" even at this early stage.

See if he is happy to float with you supporting his head. This is not unusual for small babies. They stop floating so well once they can sit up because they try to sit up in the water.

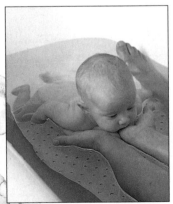

Holding the baby under her arms, with your wrists together to support her chin and keep her face out of the water, you can lay her on her front and gently glide her backwards and forwards. Don't insist on doing this if she dislikes going on her front.

A young child can be encouraged in her bath play by sharing a bath with an older child. You will need to supervise even more closely than usual, of course, and it may be safer to avoid a shared bath at the stage when a baby is learning to stand up.

Blowing bubbles

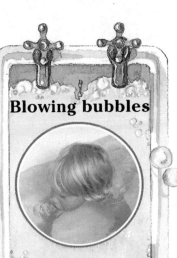

Bathtime is a good opportunity for practicing blowing bubbles. This is a very important skill as it is the first stage in learning to breathe correctly when swimming. There is more about this, including how to teach your child to blow bubbles, on page 22.

Once your child has grasped the idea of blowing bubbles on the surface of the water, try to persuade her to blow with her face submerged. To encourage her to keep her eyes open underwater, make a game of picking up small objects from the bottom of the bath.

11

FIRST TIME IN THE POOL

Make sure you are well prepared for your first trip to the pool.

It can feel like a very big step from preparing for swimming to actually getting in the water. Go on a day when you have plenty of time and both you and your child are in good form. Don't go when your child is tired or hungry, or for an hour after a meal or feeding.

Remember that your main aim is simply to get your child to enjoy herself in the water. Don't try to do too much, or stay in too long. Make a mental list of the things you want to do in the water so you don't find yourself just standing around. Ideas for introductory activities are given on pages 16-17.

Hygiene

Make sure that costumes and trunks are clean before you go swimming. Clean a baby's bottom thoroughly before you put his pants on and wipe his nose if necessary. Check that hands, faces and knees are clean and, if a child is very dirty, give him a shower. Get children to blow their noses and go to the toilet, and make sure they don't have sweets or gum in their mouths – besides being unhygienic, they could choke on them. Toddlers and older children should walk through the footbath with you.

Clean your baby's bottom before you take him into the water.

Once you are in the water, respond quickly to requests to go to the toilet and, if a baby shows signs of passing a stool, get out immediately.

After swimming, everyone should go in the shower to rinse off the chemicals in the water as these can irritate the skin. It is not necessary to use soap though. It is important to dry the ears particularly carefully after swimming. Let water drain from the ears by tilting the head first to one side for a few seconds, then to the other. Then dry with a towel.

Nervous children

Don't be too disappointed if your child refuses to get in the water even after you have followed the advice on page 7 about going to the pool previously just to watch. Don't force her in but continue to let her watch from the poolside. Walk around and point out other children enjoying themselves but never try to shame her into going in by comparing her with them unfavorably. Encourage her to sit on the edge and dangle her feet in the water with you.

12 Don't force your child to get in if she is afraid of the water.

If this situation persists for several sessions, it may just be worth trying to get in the water anyway. If the child is still very frightened however, it may be best to give up the idea of swimming for a few months, then try again.

How long to stay in

 Note the time when you get in.

This depends on the temperature of the water, the age of the child and on how much she is enjoying herself. It is important to build up the length of time you stay in the water gradually over several weeks. Don't extend the maximum times given below. Even if a child is happy in the water, there is a risk of her getting chilled or overtired.

If ever your child is cold and shivering let her get out right away. Always wrap babies and young children in a towel immediately and dry and dress them before you get changed yourself. Dress them extra-warmly and put something on their heads in cool weather.

Age of child	Maximum on 1st visit	Maximum after several visits
0-6 months	10 minutes	30 minutes
6-18 months	15 minutes	30 minutes
18 months-3 years	20 minutes	40 minutes
3 years and older	30 minutes	45 minutes (no more than 30 to be spent working hard)

Using armbands

The advantages and disadvantages of using armbands are given on page 6. Whatever you decide, it is important not to overuse armbands. They should really only be worn for a few minutes in the middle of a session to let the child enjoy a little freedom of movement. It is much better for children's confidence if they enter and leave the water without armbands and they should never wear them for a whole session.

To put armbands on without a lot of pulling and tugging, partially inflate them first, then put them in position above the child's elbow and inflate them fully. They need to be well inflated for babies and small children so they cannot slip off.

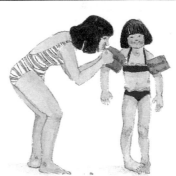

Finish inflating armbands once they are in position.

Safety

It is vital that you never leave a baby or toddler unattended at the pool, even for a moment, in or out of the water. Don't even turn your back on them.

Children who cannot swim should be watched just as closely in the water and on the poolside and even those who can swim need close supervision.

Teach children from the start that they must never run along the poolside, push people, jump in too close to them, splash them, grab hold of them or try to dunk them. Be strict about this.

Watch your child closely, even if he can swim.

13

How to get into the water

The ideal way to get into the pool with a baby is to give him to someone else to hold while you get in and then have them pass him in to you. If there is no one else available, you can try these ways, depending on the age of your baby.

Pools with a ladder

Put arm across baby's body.

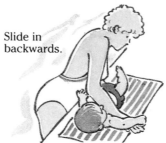

Slide in backwards.

Lift child in.

Lay your baby on a towel beside the pool. Sit down, keeping hold of him with one hand.

With one arm across his body to stop him rolling, turn and slide into the water.

When your feet are firmly on the bottom, lift him in to join you.

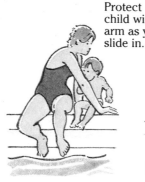

Protect child with arm as you slide in.

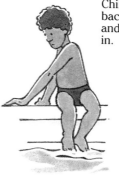

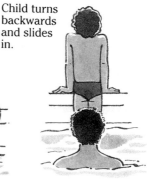

Child turns backwards and slides in.

With a baby who can sit up or a young child, you can slide in as shown here, putting one arm across him.

With a young child who can manage the ladder, climb down yourself first, back to the water, then help her down the same way.

From the age of about three, you can start encouraging a child to slide into the water.

Get in yourself first, so you can help him, especially if he is too small to touch the bottom.

Pools with shallow steps or a slope

With a baby, just walk straight into the pool, holding her securely. Slide your feet along the bottom so you don't slip.

Let a toddler or older child walk in, holding your hand and sliding her feet along the bottom. As she gains confidence over the sessions, encourage her to walk in without holding hands.

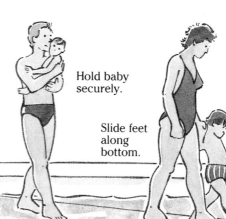

Hold baby securely.

Slide feet along bottom.

Jumping in

This is a great confidence-builder which you can start teaching even a young baby, once he has been to the pool a few times and is happy in the water.

Start by sitting your baby on the edge of the pool. From about a year you can stand him on the edge, but continue to hold him under his arms, not by his hands, or there will be too much pressure on his shoulder joints.

Lift baby in.

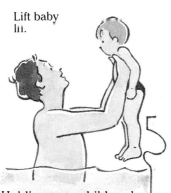

Turn him on to his front.

Glide him back to the edge.

Holding your child under his arms, lift him into the water, so that it comes up to his shoulders. To make it more fun you can sing *Humpty Dumpty* while you do this. As soon as he is in the water, turn him on his front and glide him back to the side, showing him how to grasp the rail or trough. This is important for safety as it will condition him always to make for the edge after jumping or falling into water. When he is used to being lifted in and provided he knows how to blow out into the water, you can start momentarily submerging him after lifting him in.

Jumping in on their own

Gradually, you will be able to start encouraging your child to jump in to you on his own. To begin with, you can catch him under the arms before he goes under.

Teach him to jump well out from the wall to avoid hitting it; don't let him run and jump in case he slips; and continue always to glide him back to the rail after his jump, until he can swim back on his own.

15

First activities in the water

The activities described on this and the opposite page are all aimed at getting children to relax in the water and enjoy themselves. It is a good idea to use them at the start of each session. Singing favorite songs and reciting nursery rhymes can be especially useful for putting children at ease.

These activities will probably be enough for a baby's or nervous child's first visit; with an older toddler or child who takes to the water easily, you may want to go on to a few of the activities described on pages 18-20.

Most children are not tall enough to stand in the pool, even the training pool, until they are about three, which means they are unlikely to be able to do the walking, running and jumping activities described opposite until then. If your child can touch the bottom on her first visit, encourage her to stand from the start.

It will help to give your child confidence, if you always keep your face on a level with hers. With a baby or toddler, this will probably mean your kneeling on the pool bottom. When a child is tall enough to stand, you will probably be able to squat. Remember always to maintain eye contact, smile and talk reassuringly.

Sinking and bobbing

Holding a baby close, or a child who is standing by the hands, gently sink down until your shoulders are in the water. Rise and sink again, so the child gets used to the water lapping round her shoulders. Then bob gently up and down, first on the spot, then moving around the pool.

Bouncing

If the child is happy, start bouncing him gently up and down, holding him close to start with, further away as confidence increases. Try singing *Pop goes the weasel* as you do this, with a big lift in the air on *pop* and a gentle splash down on *weasel;* or try *One potato, two potato,* lifting on *seven* and splashing down on *more.* (See page 63 for the words.) Make the splash very gentle at first.

16

Trickling water on head and face

When he is used to water on his body, gently trickle water over the back of his head, then, if he likes it, let a few drops run over his face. Don't splash him or you will put him off. You can do this while you sing *It's raining, it's pouring* or *Doctor Foster went to Gloucester* (see page 63).

Blowing bubbles

This is the first stage in learning to breathe correctly when swimming and so is an important skill, besides being fun. See page 22 for more about it. Don't press your child to put his face in the water in the early sessions; just encourage him if he does so spontaneously.

Toys

Take along one or two favorite bath toys and see if your baby will pat them along. Older babies and toddlers might like to "wash" themselves with a sponge or pour water over themselves from a container.

Walking, running and jumping

Encourage a child tall enough to stand to walk across the pool holding your hand and sliding her feet along the bottom. Then try running across or, pretending to be a kangaroo, jumping across.

Songs

Action songs can often encourage children to do things in the water they might otherwise be reluctant to do, such as getting their faces wet. They are used a lot in baby and parent classes like the one shown here. Try some of the songs suggested on page 63.

17

GETTING AFLOAT

As soon as your child is happy in the water, you can start thinking about getting him afloat. Some children are confident enough to get into a horizontal position on their very first visit to the pool but most prefer to remain upright for the first sessions.

Don't try to hurry your child. Just start each session with the introductory activities described on the previous two pages and remember that children feel more confident if you keep down to their level, maintain eye contact and smile and talk reassuringly.

Supporting your child on her front

A young baby without much control of his head will need you to keep his face out of the water. Hold him under his arms, with your wrists together to support his chin. Then move backwards, telling him to kick.

As he gains strength in his neck, support him under his arms only. Keep him low in the water so that he can feel its buoyancy, not just your support. His chin should rest on the surface of the water.

From about a year old, as the baby gains strength and confidence, you can reduce your support to holding her by her upper arms and then by her forearms, as you walk backwards encouraging kicking.

As confidence increases still further, hold her hands as you move backwards. Hold them down in the water or she will not be supported adequately and there will be too much pressure on her shoulder joints.

A child can also be encouraged to get afloat by holding the rail or trough at the edge of the pool and lifting her legs. You may need to put your hand under her tummy at first. Encourage her to kick.

From about a year and a half you can also try giving your child a float to hold under each arm. To begin with, you may need to give added support under her forearms as you walk backwards.

Kicking

Most babies and young children will kick quite spontaneously in the water but if yours does not, try kicking his legs for him to give him the idea.

Rest the top of his body against your chest and shoulder, then stretch your arms under his tummy, if he is on his front, or his bottom, if he is on his back, and hold his legs. Move his legs up and down, repeating the word "kick", as you walk backwards across the pool. There is no need to worry about the style of a child's kick at this stage.

Baby rests against chest.

Kick baby's legs for him.

Supporting your child on his back

Most young babies respond best to being put on their backs in the water. Support him under his head and bottom and, when he seems secure, gently take away the hand under his bottom. He will probably float quite happily. Some young babies can even float momentarily without any support at all but have your hands ready to take over again. Gently move sideways, supporting either with both or one hand.

Once the baby can sit up, he will probably object to being put on his back in the water. To make him feel more secure, let him rest his head on your shoulder, with his face against your cheek and his ears out of the water. Hold him under his arms or, for even greater security, stretch your arms out underneath his body and hold his legs. Move backwards through the water, telling the baby to kick.

You may encourage a toddler or child to lie back in the water if you stand up as you support her under her arms and make a game of looking at her upside down. Walk backwards, encouraging kicking.

From about a year and a half, see if your child will lie back and kick her legs, holding a float under each arm. Give added support under her shoulders at first, if she wants it.

19

Encouraging arm movement

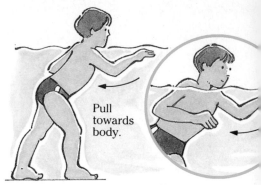

Pull towards body.

The best way to encourage arm movement in a baby is to put a brightly colored toy in front of him and get him to stretch out for it. Hold him under his arms, with your fingers outstretched to support his chin if necessary. Remember to keep him low in the water so that he can feel its buoyancy.

From about nine months old, you can try standing at the baby's side and moving his hands in a "dog paddle" action so that he gets the idea of stretching and pulling. Remember to keep his hands in the water.

A child who is tall enough can stand or walk in the water to practice the action.

Pushing and gliding

This is a useful skill as it encourages the horizontal, streamlined body position which will be needed later to swim good strokes. It also allows even quite young children the freedom of moving through the water unaided for a few seconds.

Push and glide between two people

You can do this with babies and children of all ages from the time they can hold their head up. Don't force your child though, if she does not enjoy the sensation.

Keep low down, baby's chin on water.

Keep hold of him to begin with.

Supporting under the arms, with the baby's chin on the water, one person glides him smoothly to another, who is standing a few paces away ready to take him gently again under the arms. Don't actually let go at this stage.

Remember to keep down to the baby's level, smile encouragingly, and let him know that something is about to happen, perhaps by saying "ready, steady, go" before you glide.

Once the baby or child has grasped the idea of blowing out into the water (see page 22), you can encourage him to put his face in the water during the glide if he has not already done so.

The next stage is to let him go for a moment just before the change-over. As he gets older and his leg and arm movements get stronger, you can gradually increase the length of time you let go for and the distance between the two adults so that he "swims" between you.

Push and glide from the rail

You may be able to start this from about the age of two. The child holds the rail or trough with both hands, puts his feet on the wall and then pushes off and glides towards you. He will probably want you to catch him straightaway to begin with but you will gradually be able to increase the distance you stand from the rail.

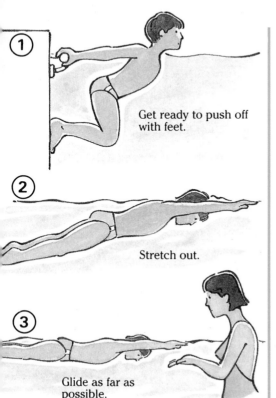

Get ready to push off with feet.

Stretch out.

Glide as far as possible.

Encourage him to stretch out with his hands together and eventually to put his face in the water.

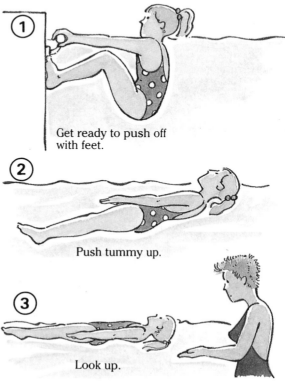

Get ready to push off with feet.

Push tummy up.

Look up.

Encourage her to look up, stretch and push her tummy up.

Push and glide to the rail

Gently glide an older baby or young child to the rail from about half a metre (2ft approx.) away, encouraging her to take hold of it. Don't let go of her until you are sure she knows how to grasp it.

When a child is tall enough, she can push off from the pool bottom and glide to the rail. Encourage her to stretch out like Superman, put her face in the water and gradually increase her distance.

Breathing

Learning how to breathe, that is breathing out when your face is in the water and in when it is out of the water, is an essential part of learning to swim.

Blowing bubbles

This is the best way of learning how to breathe out. First, blow gently in your child's face to show him what to do.

Then put your mouth on the surface of the water and blow again. Encourage your baby to copy you.

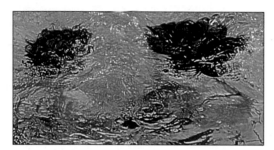

Once he can blow bubbles on the surface, encourage him to go under doing the same thing. Gently sink down together just under the surface, then come straight up again. If he splutters, just reassure him and tell him how well he has done.

Don't insist on submerging if your child really hates it. It is best to do it only once or twice each session in any case. An older child who is apprehensive about putting her face in the water may be willing to do it little by little.

Learning to put your feet back down

This is important for safety. Show your child how to do it when he is tall enough.

Be ready to hold his hands if necessary.

He should lift his head, tuck his knees up and press down with his hands.

This will bring him into an upright position.

He can then put his feet down, using his arms to help him balance.

Deep dunking

A few extreme methods of teaching advocate frequent or deep dunking. These are best avoided for various reasons.

Going too deep in the water can put a dangerous amount of pressure on a young child's ears. The pressure on a baby's ears of going down to a depth of 1m (3ft) is equivalent to that on an adult going down to 5m (16ft) – a deep diving pit. Some doctors think that frequent submerging may increase the risk of ear infections.

It can be dangerous for a child to swallow a very large amount of water and frequent submerging may have long-term psychological effects which are not immediately apparent.

Lastly, these methods are unnecessary as human beings do not normally swim underwater but along the surface.

Babies who swim underwater

It is true that children who swim unaided before the age of about three will do so just under the surface. A child should not be discouraged from doing this, but you will have to watch her very closely and help her to come to the surface for air. Signs of needing to take a breath include shaking her head or moving her arms and legs faster. Guide her to the surface immediately, holding her under her arms or chin. Eventually she will learn to surface on her own.

"Motor boats"

Encourage your child to blow bubbles with his face in the water by getting him to push and glide and make an engine noise.

Opening the eyes underwater

Ask your child if she can see you when you submerge together, or hold colorful objects low in the water or put them on the pool bottom for her to pick up.

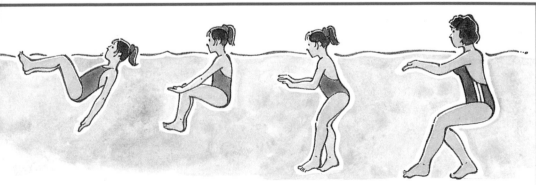

After pressing down with her hands, she lifts her head and tucks her knees up.

Her hands sweep forwards and up, palms facing up, as she becomes upright.

She can then put her feet down, using her arms for balance.

Be ready to support her shoulders gently if necessary.

23

Turning over in the water

This is a good confidence-building skill and can be useful if a child is not especially happy in a certain position.

Hold your child under the arms, standing at the side, if he is on his front, behind his head, if he is on his back, and gently roll him over. He may like to pretend to be a sausage frying in a pan while you do this or have you sing *There were ten in the bed,* rolling him over on *roll over.* (See page 63 for the words.) Eventually, he will learn to turn himself over.

The shallow water method

This can be a useful method of learning to swim because it gives children a lot of confidence, but you need to have water which is no deeper than 30-45cm (12-18in). The sea can be an ideal place to learn to swim in this way.

The idea is that children walk their hands along the bottom while kicking their legs and, as confidence increases, begin to take their hands off the bottom too.

Points to remember

- Always plan ahead carefully: where and when to go, what to take, what to do in the water.
- Get your baby used to the big bath at home before going to the pool.
- Be conscious of safety the whole time.
- Don't force or hurry your child. Reassure him and keep down to his level.
- Start the session with gentle warm-up activities.
- When your child is used to being upright in the water, get him to lie down while you move him along.
- Give instructions about kicking even to young babies.
- Get him used to water on his head and face.
- Teach him to blow bubbles so he learns to breathe out into the water.
- Try to limit your use of armbands.
- Don't stay in too long.

When to start proper strokes

It is important not to try to rush your child through the stages of learning to swim or to start teaching him to do the proper strokes too soon. Always remember that your main aim is for your child to enjoy the water.

Don't worry if you think his progress is slow. Children vary in the rate at which they learn to swim just as they do in other aspects of development and just because a child is a slow starter does not mean that he will not be a competent swimmer later on. Children do not have the strength to swim on the surface of the water until they are about three. Then, they may be able to do a dog paddle type of stroke on their front and swim on their back with their arms out to the side. Before a child starts to learn the major strokes (front crawl, back crawl and breast stroke), he should be able to swim at least ten metres (about 11 yards) on his own and be happy doing all of the activities described so far in this book.

Some children may be able to start the strokes as early as age four or five though it is unusual for a child to have the strength or comprehension level to do them properly before he is six or seven. At the same time as children start learning the strokes, they can be introduced to other water skills as well. The strokes are described on pages 26-43 and further water skills on pages 44-50.

Your child will need to have the strokes and skills demonstrated to him. If you are not a good enough swimmer yourself, find someone else he can watch and go through the pictures in this book with him.

You may also want to start thinking about classes. Many pools hold classes for children without their parents from the age of three.*

Planning a session

Once you start teaching your child the strokes, don't forget that swimming should always be fun. Continue to start the session with introductory activities of the type shown on pages 16-17; don't spend more than a third of the session on one particular stroke, remember to introduce a contrasting water skill too and leave time for just playing around at the end of the session.

Here is just one possible way of breaking up the time in a 30 minute session:

1 Discuss with your child what you are going to do.

1 minute

2 Do some introductory activities (see pages 16-24) and/or swim a stroke your child already knows, say front crawl.

4 minutes

3 Learn a new stroke, say back crawl.

10 minutes

4 Introduce a contrasting water skill, say treading water, and practice previously learned strokes and skills.

10 minutes

5 Play time. Let your child do what he likes but remember to watch him closely and give help when necessary.

5 minutes

*Find out what classes are available from the pools, the library or the local council.

FRONT CRAWL

Front crawl is the easiest stroke to teach and learn.

Be sure to build up the stroke in stages.

Front crawl is the fastest and most efficient swimming stroke. It is also the easiest to teach and learn and so is a good stroke to start with. It follows naturally from the dog paddle that children use when they first start swimming. However, for children who are still not keen on putting their faces in the water, breast stroke or back crawl may be a better choice of first stroke.

It is important to build up the stroke gradually, making sure your child has mastered each stage before going on to the next. First concentrate on the body position, then practice the leg kick, then add the arm action and finally the breathing. To maintain interest, though, always let your child try the whole stroke at the start and end of the practice.

Remember, if you can't demonstrate the stroke yourself, find someone else your child can watch and look at the pictures in this book together. Remember, too, not to spend more than a third of the session on one particular stroke. See page 25 for ideas on using the rest of the time in the session.

Body position

The body should be streamlined and stretched, and as flat as possible. The arm action and breathing will cause a certain amount of body roll but this should not be too exaggerated.

The head should be in a natural position, neither lifted, nor buried. If it is lifted, the hips and legs will drop too low; if it is buried, they will be raised too high. The water-line should be between the nose and hair-line; the eyes should look forward and down, and ideally be kept open.

Body position practices

- Push and glide from the pool bottom holding a float out in front, face in the water.
- Push and glide from the pool bottom without a float, face in the water.

Foot only just breaks surface of water.

Feet extended but relaxed.

Foot should not go much lower than body depth.

26

Leg action

The legs should stabilize the body and provide some forward movement, though most of this comes from the arms.

The legs should kick up and down, alternately and continuously, keeping close together. The movement must start at the hips and end with a whip-like action of the foot. The legs should be kept straight with the feet extended but relaxed. The foot should not go much deeper than the depth of the body on the down-kick and should only just break the surface of the water on the up-kick, making a small splash.

Children usually do six leg kicks per arm cycle but this is not important and they will not be able to count them anyway. The opposite leg kicks down at the start of the arm pull, as this helps to balance the body.

Leg action practices

- Kicking at the rail.

- Kicking, holding a float under each arm.

- Kicking, holding a float out in front, chin on the water.

- Kicking, holding a float out in front, face in the water.

- Kicking, arms outstretched, face in the water.

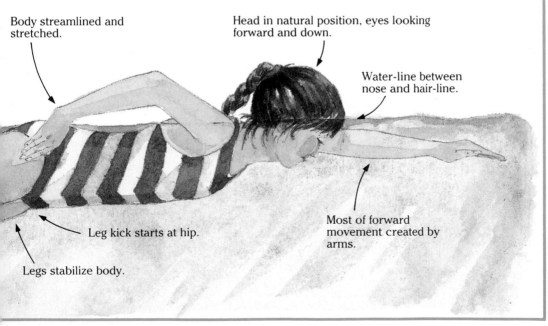

Body streamlined and stretched.

Head in natural position, eyes looking forward and down.

Water-line between nose and hair-line.

Leg kick starts at hip.

Most of forward movement created by arms.

Legs stabilize body.

Arm action

Most of the forward movement in front crawl comes from the arm action. This is continuous and alternate, one arm pulling while the other recovers.

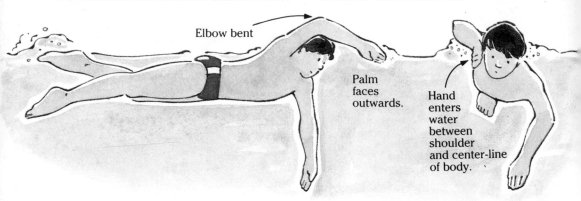

Elbow bent

Palm faces outwards.

Hand enters water between shoulder and center-line of body.

The arm enters the water thumb first, with the elbow bent, the fingers together and the palm of the hand facing diagonally outwards. It should enter the water between the shoulder and the center-line of the body.

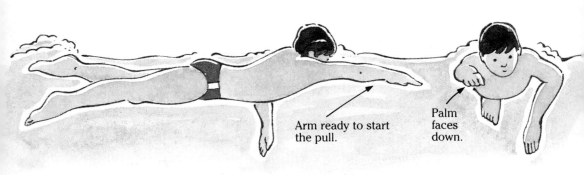

Arm ready to start the pull.

Palm faces down.

As the wrist and forearm follow the hand into the water and completely submerge, the elbow straightens and the forearm rotates so that the palm is facing down and slightly backwards ready to pull towards the feet.

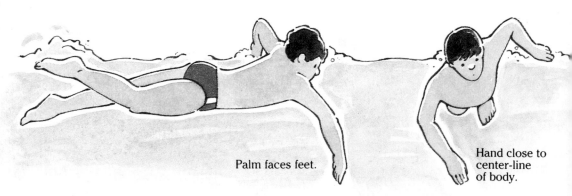

Palm faces feet.

Hand close to center-line of body.

The arm pulls down and back, with the hand keeping close to the center-line of the body, the palm facing the feet. The elbow bends again. The elbow must be kept high to ensure that the water is pushed backwards and not downwards.

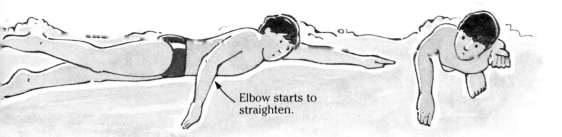

Elbow starts to straighten.

The hand continues under the body, palm still facing the feet, and pushes back towards the thigh, with the elbow gradually straightening. By the time the thumb reaches the thigh, the elbow is almost completely straight.

Elbow leaves water first.

The elbow bends again and is the first part of the arm to leave the water. The arm then swings forwards quickly but in a relaxed way. This is a non-productive part of the stroke, so as little time and energy as possible should be used on it.

Arm action practices

- Practice the action standing on the poolside, leaning forward slightly.

- Practice the action walking in shallow water.

- Practice the action standing in shallow water as shown above.

- Push and glide from the side or pool bottom, start to kick legs and then introduce one or two arm cycles. Increase the number of arm cycles as the stroke improves.

29

Breathing

Action. Breathing should be blended into the stroke with as little interference as possible. The action should be smooth and unhurried.

Breathing out takes place gradually through the nose and mouth, while the face is submerged.

As one arm starts to recover, the head turns, ready to breathe in.

As the arm swings forward, the breath is taken, underneath it.

The head should be back in its normal position before the hand enters the water.

The head should turn like a door knob. It does not need to be lifted because the forward motion of the body creates a trough to breathe in.

Common faults

Most of these arise from trying to build up the stroke too fast, without mastering each stage in turn.

When you are correcting your child, always keep your instructions as simple and concise as possible. As you will see from the checklist below, sometimes the corrections need to be exaggerated.

Always make sure your child can watch the correct action being demonstrated and show him the pictures in this book.

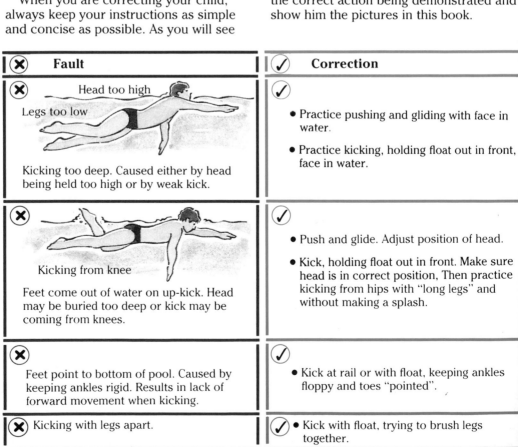

✖ **Fault**	✓ **Correction**
✖ Head too high Legs too low Kicking too deep. Caused either by head being held too high or by weak kick.	✓ • Practice pushing and gliding with face in water. • Practice kicking, holding float out in front, face in water.
✖ Kicking from knee Feet come out of water on up-kick. Head may be buried too deep or kick may be coming from knees.	✓ • Push and glide. Adjust position of head. • Kick, holding float out in front. Make sure head is in correct position, Then practice kicking from hips with "long legs" and without making a splash.
✖ Feet point to bottom of pool. Caused by keeping ankles rigid. Results in lack of forward movement when kicking.	✓ • Kick at rail or with float, keeping ankles floppy and toes "pointed".
✖ Kicking with legs apart.	✓ • Kick with float, trying to brush legs together.

Timing

Once the stroke is mastered, it is best to breathe on both sides, every third arm pull. If a breath is always taken on the same side, the body position is more likely to become unbalanced. Breathing on both sides also has the advantage of letting the swimmer see what is happening to either side of him.

Breathing practices

- With one hand on rail, the other lower down on wall, practice turning head while kicking.
- Practice arm action standing or walking in shallow water and include turn of head on every third arm pull.

- Practice turning head to breathe while kicking holding a float.
- Practice full stroke, first holding breath, then breathing occasionally, then gradually increasing number of breaths taken.

 Hand enters water across center-line of body so that swimmer "snakes" up pool.	• Arm action practices, aiming to enter water with hand wide of shoulder.
Slapping water with hand.	• Arm action practices, with emphasis on "spearing" water with hand and putting thumb in water first.
 Pulling too deeply with straight arm resulting in lack of power in arm action.	• Arm action practices, concentrating on keeping elbow high and gradually bending it.
Not pushing with arm, only pulling. Results in lack of power.	• Arm action practices, concentrating on pushing right through to thigh.
Not keeping palm facing feet, or forgetting to keep fingers together. Results in lack of power.	• Arm action practices, emphasizing "catching" or "fastening on to" water with palm and fingers before start of pull.
 Recovering with hand too high.	• Arm action practices, emphasizing that elbow leaves water first and remains higher than hand as arm swings forward.
Lifting head to breathe.	• Breathing practices, emphasizing that head should turn like a door knob and one ear should stay in water.

BACK CRAWL

Back crawl is a useful stroke for anyone who dislikes putting their face in the water, or finds the breathing technique required for front crawl difficult, though some people are put off by not being able to see where they are going. It is an easy stroke to teach and learn once the body position has been mastered. The action is basically an upside-down front crawl.

Back crawl is a good stroke for people who dislike putting their face in the water.

Body position

The body should be streamlined and stretched, and as flat as possible. Beginners sometimes tend to try to sit up in the water but this must be avoided.

The head should be kept still and in line with the body throughout the stroke. The ears should be submerged and the eyes should look up and slightly forward towards the feet.

The top part of the body will roll to the side of the pulling arm. This is a natural part of the stroke. The arm action will also make the hips sway from side to side, though this movement should be kept to a minimum by the leg action.

Body position practices

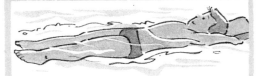

- Push and glide from pool bottom, holding a float on tummy.
- Push and glide from poolside without float.

- Push and glide with float held behind head. (Use this for a child who is nervous of lying back in the water).

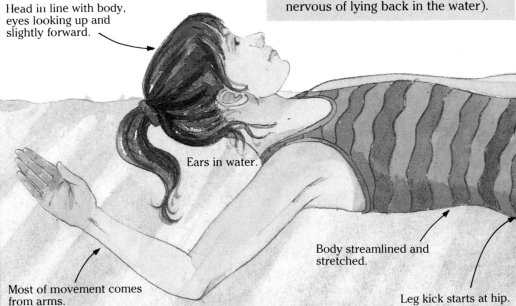

Head in line with body, eyes looking up and slightly forward.

Ears in water.

Most of movement comes from arms.

Body streamlined and stretched.

Leg kick starts at hip.

Remember that it is important for your child to see the correct stroke demonstrated; be sure that she builds up the stroke gradually, mastering the body position first, then the leg action, then the arm action and finally the breathing; and don't let her spend more than a third of the session practicing the stroke.

Make sure your child sees the correct stroke demonstrated.

Leg action

As in front crawl, the main function of the legs is to stabilize the body rather than to provide movement.

The legs kick up and down, alternately and continuously, keeping close together. The movement starts at the hips and ends with a whip-like action of the foot. The legs should be kept straight with the feet extended but relaxed. The foot should not go much deeper than the depth of the body on the down-kick and should only just break the surface of the water on the up-kick, making a small splash.

Again as in front crawl, there are usually six leg kicks to each arm cycle, with the opposite leg kicking down at the start of each arm pull to balance the body. This usually comes naturally as the stroke improves.

Leg action practices

- Kicking, holding a float under each arm.
- For a timid child, kicking, holding float behind head.
- Kicking, holding float over tummy.
- Kicking, while sculling with hands (see page 44 for how to scull).

- Kicking, with hands on thighs.

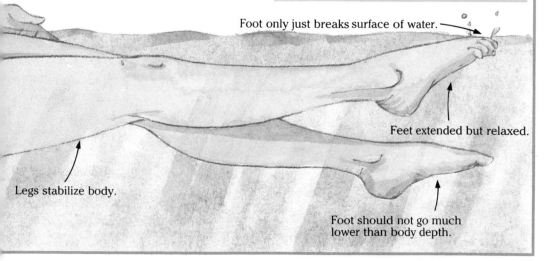

Foot only just breaks surface of water.

Feet extended but relaxed.

Legs stabilize body.

Foot should not go much lower than body depth.

Arm action

As in front crawl, most of the movement comes from the arms. Again, the action is continuous and alternate, one arm pulling while the other recovers.

There are two types of arm action: the straight arm pull and the bent arm pull. The straight arm pull is often used by beginners and people who swim just for fun. The bent arm pull is faster and more powerful, and is used by competitive swimmers and any beginners to whom it comes naturally.

The pull you show your child will obviously depend on which one you do yourself. If she is over the age of about six, it may be worth trying to show her the stronger, bent arm pull from the start. If one type of action comes more easily to her than the other, let her concentrate on that.

Start of pull

Hand directly behind shoulder.

Palm faces outwards.

Both pulls start in the same way. With the arm and hand in a straight line, the arm enters the water directly in line with the shoulder, little finger first, palm facing outwards and fingers together. There should be very little or no splash. The hand then "fastens on to" the water, ready to start the pull.

Straight arm pull

Arm pulls out to side.

Arm straight

The arm remains straight and starts to pull outwards and slightly downwards.

Hand should not go below body depth.

The hand reaches its lowest point at the end of the pull, when it is level with the shoulder. It should not go below body depth.

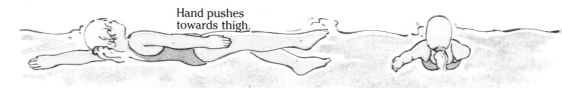

Hand pushes towards thigh.

The hand continues its semi-circular pathway, pushing inwards towards the hips. The arm remains straight.

Bent arm pull

Elbow bent

The hand starts to pull towards the feet. As it does so, the elbow bends and the palm starts to come into position facing the feet.

Bend at elbow approx. 90°.

Fingers point upwards.

By the end of the pull, when the shoulder, elbow and hand are level, the bend at the elbow is about 90°. The other arm is recovering.

Arm straight

Hand flicks down to pool bottom.

The hand now pushes towards the feet and the elbow gradually straightens. The movement ends with a flick of the hand down to the pool bottom. This has the effect of raising the shoulder in preparation for the arm leaving the water.

End of pull

Arm almost brushes ear.

Hand above shoulder.

Both pulls end in the same way. The arm is lifted smoothly out of the water, straight, with wrist relaxed and the palm facing the thigh. As it swings back over the head, almost brushing the ear, the wrist turns so that the palm is facing outwards ready to re-enter the water.

35

Arm action practices

- Practice arm action standing on poolside.

- Practice arm action with feet hooked under rail.
- Push and glide from side or pool bottom, start to kick legs and then introduce one or two arm cycles. Increase number of arm cycles as stroke improves.

Breathing

Beginners sometimes tend to hold their breath so you may need to remind your child to breathe normally and regularly. As the stroke improves, encourage her to take a complete breath every stroke cycle.

Breathing practice

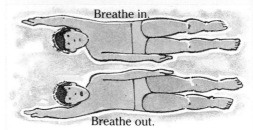

Breathe in.

Breathe out.

- Do the full stroke, breathing in on one arm pull, out on the other.

Common faults

Remember that the best way to avoid faults creeping in is always to master the stroke in stages. Keep any corrections you have to make clear and simple, exaggerating where necessary, and let your child see the correct stroke demonstrated.

❌ Fault	✓ Correction
 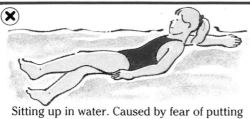 Sitting up in water. Caused by fear of putting head back. Results in head being too high and legs too low.	 • Push and glide practices. Concentrate on putting head back and ears in water. Look up and push tummy up. • Kick, holding float behind head.
  Putting head too far back. Usually caused by trying to look ahead. Results in legs being too high in water.	✓ • Kick, holding float behind head. Put chin on chest and look at fixed point on poolside.
 Kicking from knees.	✓ • Kick, holding float over thighs. Concentrate on kicking from hips with "long legs". Knees should not press against float.

✖	✔
Kicking with stiff ankles.	• Kick, holding float over tummy, keeping ankles floppy and toes "pointed".
Kicking with a lot of splash.	• Kick with float over tummy. Concentrate on stretching out, putting head back and keeping legs under surface of water.
Putting back of hand, instead of little finger, into the water first.	• Practice arm action standing on poolside. • For a short distance, try doing arm action with one arm only, holding float under other arm and kicking legs.
Hand enters water too wide of shoulder.	• Practice arm action standing on poolside. • Do a few strokes aiming to enter water with hand across center of head.
Hand enters water across center of head.	• Practice arm action on poolside. • Do a few strokes aiming to enter water with hand wide of shoulder.
Pulling too deeply. Causes bobbing up and down.	• Do a few strokes concentrating hard on not letting arm go below body depth.
Arm not leaving water thumb first and bending during recovery.	• Practice arm action on poolside. • Practice with one arm only for a short distance, holding float under other arm.

BREAST STROKE

Beginners can swim breast stroke with their chin on the water.

This is a popular stroke with people who swim just for fun. Breathing need not be a problem as it is possible to swim the stroke keeping your face out of the water all the time, and you can see where you are going. Breast stroke is essential for survival swimming because it is less tiring to swim over long distances than other strokes and it is used for life-saving. Remember that it is important for your child to see the correct stroke demonstrated. Be sure that she builds up the stroke gradually, mastering the body position first, then the leg action, then the arm action and finally the breathing; until her arms and legs are working well together, she should swim breast stroke with her chin on the water. Don't let her spend more than a third of the session practicing the stroke.

Body position

The body should be as flat and streamlined as possible. It is harder to achieve this position in breast stroke than in front crawl because the head has to be lifted to breathe and the heels should not break the surface of the water during the leg kick. This means that the body is inevitably at more of a slant. The aim is to keep the slant as slight as possible in order to keep water resistance to a minimum.

The two sides of the body should be kept symmetrical throughout the stroke, with the shoulders parallel to the surface of the water.

The head should be kept steady and the eyes should look along or just under the surface of the water.

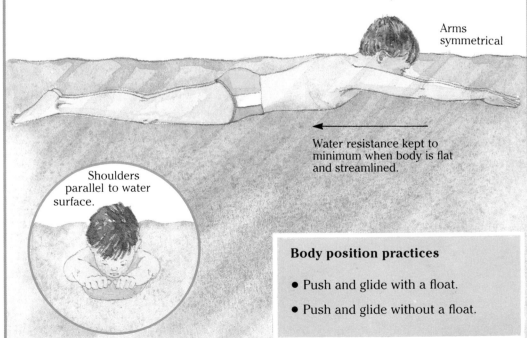

Arms symmetrical

Water resistance kept to minimum when body is flat and streamlined.

Shoulders parallel to water surface.

Body position practices

- Push and glide with a float.

- Push and glide without a float.

38

Leg action

Much of the forward movement in breast stroke comes from a strong leg kick. There are two types of leg action: the wedge kick and the whip kick.

The wedge is a slow relaxed kick used by beginners and people who swim just for fun. The whip is a faster, more powerful kick used by competitive swimmers and any beginners to whom it comes naturally.

The kick you show your child will obviously depend on which one you do yourself. If she is over the age of about six, it is probably best to show her the stronger whip kick from the start. If one type of action comes more easily to her than the other, let her concentrate on that.

The important factor in both types of kick is the position of the feet. They should be turned outwards, with the toes turned up towards the shins.

Tell your child to imagine she is holding a ball between the top of her foot and her shin.

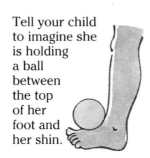

Both kicks start and end with the legs straight out behind the body, feet together and extended but relaxed.

Wedge kick

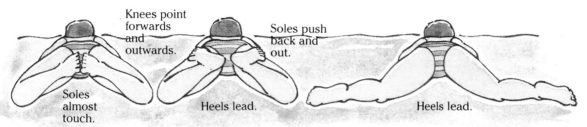

Knees point forwards and outwards.

Soles almost touch.

Soles push back and out.

Heels lead.

Heels lead.

The feet are drawn up towards the bottom with the knees pointing forwards and outwards and the soles of the feet almost touching.

With the toes turned towards the shins and the heels leading, the soles of the feet then push outwards and backwards.

The legs are straight by the end of the kick. The heels continue to lead as the legs sweep back together again behind the body.

Whip kick

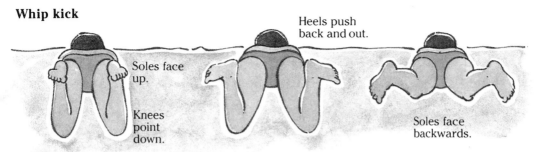

Soles face up.

Knees point down.

Heels push back and out.

Soles face backwards.

The feet are drawn up to the bottom about hip width apart with the knees pointing downwards to the pool bottom and the soles facing upwards.

With the feet turned out, toes turned towards the shins, the heels push mainly backwards and slightly outwards in a whip-like action.

As the legs straighten, the soles of the feet come into a backward-facing position. The legs are brought together again behind the body.

Leg action practices

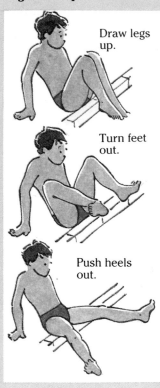

Draw legs up.

Turn feet out.

Push heels out.

- Practice leg action sitting on edge of pool. Start with legs outstretched, then draw them up. Turn feet out and toes to shins. Push out to side, heels leading, and finally bring legs back together again.

- Practice action, holding float under each arm.

- Practice action holding float out in front, chin on water.

- Practice action lying on back, with float under each arm. Get child to watch feet to make sure they are turned out.

- Practice action holding float out in front, face in water.

- Practice action with arms outstretched, face in water.

- Practice action at rail.

Arm action

The breast stroke arm action is a continuous circling movement with a short glide. There are two types of action:

the straight arm pull, done with the wedge kick and the bent arm pull, done with the whip kick (see page 39).

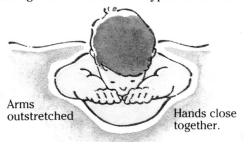

Arms outstretched

Hands close together.

Arm pull begins.

Both pulls start and end in the glide position, with the arms outstretched and the hands close together, about 15cm (6in) below the surface of the water.

The palms then turn outwards and the arms start to pull outwards, downwards and backwards until they are just beyond shoulder width apart.

40

Straight arm pull

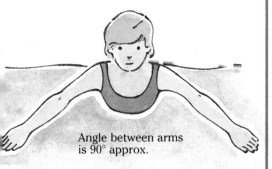

Angle between arms is 90° approx.

The arms remain almost straight and continue the pull until there is an angle of about 90° between them: that is until they are almost level with the shoulders and wide of them. At this stage the fingertips should be about 30cm (12in) below the surface.

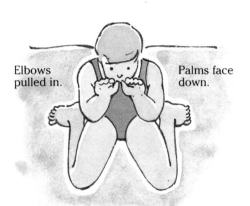

Elbows pulled in.

Palms face down.

The elbows now bend and drop, the hands are brought together with the palms facing downwards and the elbows are pulled in to the sides of the body. The arms then stretch forwards smoothly and quickly.

Arm action practices

- Practice arm action standing on poolside, bending forward slightly.
- Practice arm action standing in shallow water.
- Push and glide from side or pool bottom; with chin on water, make one arm stroke and then one leg stroke. Gradually increase number of strokes made.

Bent arm pull

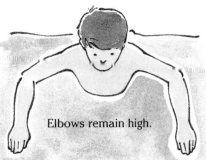

Elbows remain high.

When the hands are just beyond shoulder width apart (see illustration on opposite page, bottom right), the elbows bend but remain high while the hands pull back and down, palms facing the feet and fingers pointing to the pool bottom.

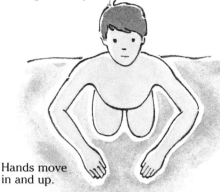

Hands move in and up.

When the hands are underneath the elbows, they start to move together again in a swirling, inwards and upwards movement. The elbows follow the hands in to the sides of the body.

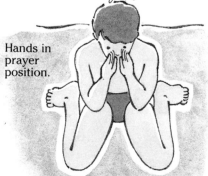

Hands in prayer position.

The palms will probably be in a prayer position or facing upwards at the end of this movement. They should be turned downwards at the start of the glide. 41

Breathing and coordination

Until she has mastered the leg and arm actions, your child should swim breast stroke with her chin on the water. This means that breathing should not be a problem, though you may have to remind her to breathe normally and not to hold her breath.

Once arms and legs are working well together, she will swim the stroke much more efficiently if she puts her face in the water for part of the stroke and so reduces the slant of her body.

The breast stroke rhythm is basically pull-breathe-kick-glide, pull-breathe-kick-glide. The action should be smooth and continuous throughout, never jerky.

Breathing and coordination practices

- Holding float out in front, with face in water, do leg action only; every few strokes, practice raising head minimally to breathe as legs are just starting to be drawn up to bottom.

- Practice full stroke with face in water, gradually increasing number of breaths taken across width of pool.

- Count how many strokes it takes to do a width of the pool and then try to reduce the number.

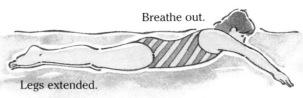

Breathe out.

Legs extended.

Breathing out should take place into the water through the mouth and nose during the glide and first part of the arm pull. When the arm pull begins the legs are fully extended.

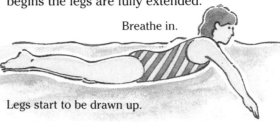

Breathe in.

Legs start to be drawn up.

As the arm pull continues, a breath is taken and the legs start to be drawn up to the bottom. The head should be raised to breathe, not by pulling the shoulders up, but just by pushing the chin forward the minimum amount necessary for the mouth to clear the water.

Hands come together in front of face.

The legs continue to be drawn up as the hands come together in front of the face.

Face back in water.

Leg kick starts.

As the arms stretch forward, the leg kick starts. The face should be back in the water.

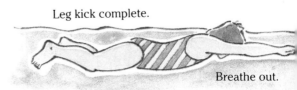

Leg kick complete.

Breathe out.

By the time the arms are fully extended, the leg kick is complete.

Common faults

Remember that the best way to avoid faults creeping in is always to master the stroke in stages. Keep any corrections you have to make clear and simple, and let your child see the correct action demonstrated.

Fault	Correction
 Water resistance Head is held too high out of water so that hips and legs are too low and body meets a lot of water resistance.	• Push and glide with chin on water. • Do breathing practices.
 Not kicking symmetrically. Caused either by moving head about or not keeping shoulders level.	• Practice leg action, first holding a float under each arm, then holding a float out in front, chin on water. Concentrate on looking ahead, keeping head steady and shoulders level. This should keep hips level. Make sure, also, that knees are bending the same amount and in the same direction.
 Pointing feet, instead of turning them out and up.	• Push and glide from rail with feet placed on wall like a frog's. • Pretend to be a frog and jump in with feet turned out. • Practice leg action lying on back, watching feet to make sure soles are pushing back. • Practice leg action holding a float under each arm or one float out in front. Concentrate on pushing back with flat feet.
Pulling too far back.	• Practice arm action standing up. Make sure movement takes place in front of shoulders and that hands are always in sight.
Bobbing up and down. Caused either by bringing knees too far under body or by lifting head too high to breathe.	• Practice leg action either with two floats or one, concentrating on bringing heels up to bottom. • Do breathing practices, concentrating on keeping head and shoulders steady and just pushing chin forward until it is on surface of water.

43

MORE WATER SKILLS

Your child can start learning the skills described on the next few pages at the same time as starting to learn the major strokes. They will provide variety and almost all of them are very useful survival skills. It is best to introduce them one at a time to prevent your child getting confused.

Sculling

This is an arm action which can be used either to keep afloat in one place or to move gently through the water.

Lie flat on your back with your arms by your sides. Keep your arms straight but relaxed with your hands in line with your forearms. Then move your arms sideways away from your body with your little fingers raised slightly so

that your palms are facing outwards and downwards. The angle of tilt should be no more than 30°.

Your hands should not move more than about 30cm (12in) away from your body before turning to come in again. On the inward movement your thumbs should be raised so that your palms face inwards and downwards.

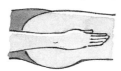

Repeat this action continuously. There should be equal pressure on both outward and inward movements and the movement should start at the shoulders.

Sculling on the spot

Palms face down.

To scull on the spot, keep your palms facing downwards.

Sculling head first

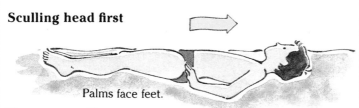

Palms face feet.

The same sculling action made with your wrists bent upwards, will make you travel head first.

Sculling feet first

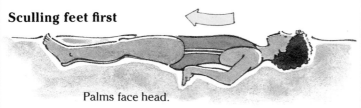

Palms face head.

To travel feet first, scull with your wrists bent downwards

Sculling practices

- Practice arm action standing on dry land.

- Practice arm action with hands resting on a flat surface at shoulder height, arms outstretched. Imagine you are trying to press a hole in sand, using your thumbs on the outward movement and your little fingers on the inward movement.

- Practice arm action standing in shoulder depth water with arms outstretched to the front and submerged. Start off slowly and build up speed.

- Start off doing the practice above, then tilt fingers upwards, lie back in water and continue sculling. Move hands so that they are alongside hips. This should produce a head-first scull.

- Start off as before, then tilt fingers downwards, lie back and continue sculling to produce a feet-first scull.

- Start off as before, then, keeping palms flat, lie back and continue sculling to produce an on-the-spot scull.

Floating

This is an energy-conserving survival skill. The floats are described below in what is generally considered to be their order of difficulty. However, floating is a fairly individual matter, depending partly on a person's build, so you may prefer to learn them in a different order. The key to successful floating is feeling confident enough to relax completely in the water. Start by practicing in shallow water so you can put your feet down quickly if necessary and, as you gain confidence, move to deeper water

Floating on your back

Lie back in the water with your arms by your sides. You may need to make gentle sculling movements to begin with until you get your balance and feel buoyant. Or, you may find it easier to float with your arms and legs in a star shape, as shown above.

Floating on your front

Take a breath in and then lie with your face in the water, either with your arms and legs outstretched or in a star shape. Lift your head to breathe as necessary.

Mushroom float

Lie on your front, take a deep breath in and then tuck up into a ball, clasping your arms round your legs.

Floating vertically

You need to practice this in fairly deep water from the start. After getting into a vertical position, simply put your head back so that your mouth and nose are just above the surface of the water.

Floating practices

- To begin with, you can try all the different ways of floating holding two floats, either at arms' length or under your arms depending on which type of float you are doing.

45

Treading water

This is another way of staying in one place while using as little energy as possible, this time in an upright position. This is useful if you are in difficulty and need to attract attention by waving.

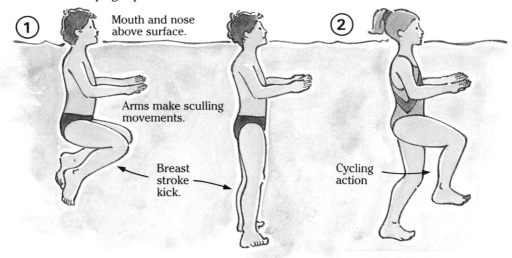

① Mouth and nose above surface.

Arms make sculling movements.

Breast stroke kick.

② Cycling action

The aim is to keep your mouth and nose above the water surface by making slow, unhurried movements. It is a waste of energy to try to hold your body high out of the water.

Your arms should make gentle sculling movements at about chest level, palms facing downwards, while your legs do either a breast stroke kick or a cycling action.

Treading water practices

- Practice leg action holding a float under each arm.
- Practice, holding on to rail or trough first with both hands, then with just one hand while the other sculls out to the side.

Conserving body heat

This can be very important if you have difficulties in cold water. You have to try to keep your internal organs warm while keeping your head above water.

Wrap your arms round your upper body and draw your knees up to protect your lower body. Some people find the position easier if they cross their lower legs. Practice with a float first, and then try without one.

Practice with a float.

Draw legs up.

Cross arms over chest.

Jumps

Once you are confident about jumping into shallow water (see page 15), you can start jumping in out of your depth so long as you know how to surface again.

The straddle and bomb jumps described below can be useful if ever you are forced to jump into water in an emergency and are not sure of its depth.

Straight jump

Jump up and out from the edge of the pool and enter the water with body erect, toes pointed and eyes looking forward.

To surface, do a strong breast stroke leg kick and press down to the pool bottom with the palms of your hands, if necessary putting your arms above your head and pulling them down strongly to your sides first.

Straddle or scissor jump

This jump should not be made from a height of more than just over a meter (4ft) above the water or it will be painful. Although it is a shallow jump, to begin with it should be practiced in water that is at least a good half meter (2ft) deeper than your height with your arms stretched above your head, to be sure of avoiding hitting the pool floor.

You should step out from the edge of the pool, rather than jump, and enter the water with one foot forward, the other back, arms spread out at shoulder level and the top part of your body leaning forward slightly. This increases the area of your body that hits the water and so prevents it sinking very far.

Once in the water, try to bring your legs together slightly and press down to the pool bottom with your palms. This will also help to stop you sinking.

Bomb jump

A bomb jump will make you go slightly deeper in the water but can be made from a greater height than the straddle jump.

As you jump or step off the edge, tuck your knees up to your chest, clasping your arms round your legs if necessary, so that your bottom hits the water first.

Surfacing is the same as for a straight jump.

47

Climbing out

For safety reasons, you should practice climbing out of the water without the help of a ladder.

Put hands on side.

Starting off in shallow water, reach up and put your hands on the poolside.

Haul self up.

Then push off from the pool bottom and haul yourself up until your arms are straight and supporting your body.

Get one knee on to side.

You can then get one knee on to the poolside and stand up.

As your arms get stronger you can practice hauling yourself up from deeper water, where you will not have the help of a push-off.

Surface diving and swimming underwater

These can be useful skills in an emergency but are more likely to be used at the swimming pool for the fun of picking things up from the pool bottom or swimming through someone's legs.

Head-first dive

Stretch out.

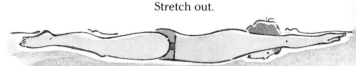

Take a deep breath in and then stretch out on your front.

Then make a quick breast stroke arm pull, at the same time bending sharply at the hips and plunging your head and shoulders forcibly downwards into the water.

As your legs start to come out of the water, straighten at the hips so that your legs are raised into the air. At the same time push your arms forwards again until they are outstretched in line with your body.

The weight of your legs will drive your body further downwards. Additional depth can be gained by making another breast stroke pull if necessary but no leg action should be made until your legs and feet are completely submerged.

To get into a more horizontal position for swimming underwater, you will then need to turn your fingers upwards.

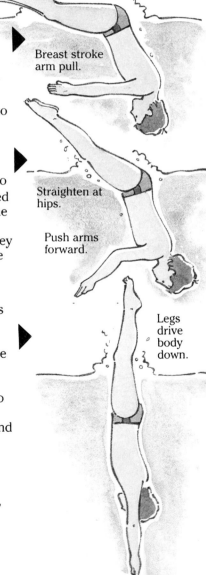

Bend at hips.

Breast stroke arm pull.

Straighten at hips.

Push arms forward.

Legs drive body down.

Feet-first dive

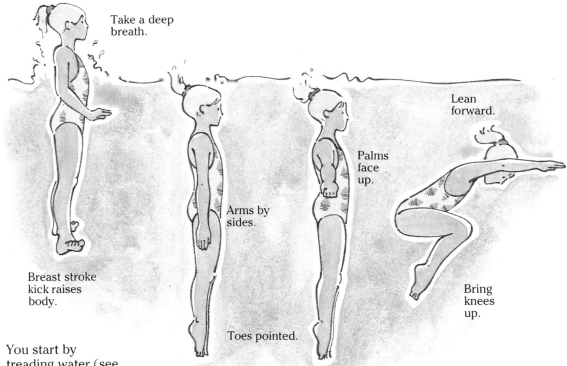

Take a deep breath.

Breast stroke kick raises body.

Arms by sides.

Toes pointed.

Palms face up.

Lean forward.

Bring knees up.

You start by treading water (see page 46), then, at the same time as taking a deep breath in, give a vigorous kick to raise your body as high out of the water as possible.

With legs together, toes pointed and arms by your sides for streamlining, let your body drop below the surface.

To get more depth sweep your hands outwards and upwards from your thighs to finish above your head.

When you are deep enough, draw your knees up to your chest, lean forward and start swimming (see below).

Swimming underwater

There are three methods of underwater swimming:

- using breast stroke arm and leg action
- using breast stroke arm action with crawl leg action
- using dog paddle arm action with crawl leg action.

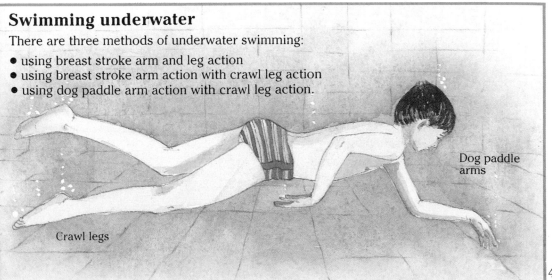

Dog paddle arms

Crawl legs

Somersaults

Besides helping to develop confidence and being great fun, turning somersaults in the water is good preparation for diving.

Forward somersault

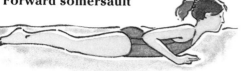

Start by lying on your front, doing an on-the-spot scull with your arms. Raise your head to breathe in.

Bring your knees up to your chest, tuck your chin down to your knees, press down with your palms and start to somersault forwards.

Make backward scooping movements to help rotate your body. Imagine you are turning a skipping rope backwards.

Keep in the tight tucked position throughout the somersault, with back rounded and toes pointed.

When your head reaches the surface, start to straighten out and scull on the spot again. Then raise your head.

Backward somersault

Start off on your back, arms doing an on-the-spot scull. Breathe in.

Bring your knees up to your chest, tuck your chin down to your knees, press down with your palms and start to somersault backwards.

Rotate your body by making forward scooping movements, as though you are turning a skipping rope forwards.

Throughout the somersault, keep in the tight tucked position.

When your lower legs reach the surface, start to straighten out and scull on the spot again.

Somersault practices

- Practice the tucked position without somersaulting.

- Push and glide from the side into a somersault.

- Breast stroke into a front somersault.

- Spring off the pool bottom into a somersault.

50

SWIMMING IN THE SEA

Provided you are extremely careful about safety, the sea can be an excellent place to learn to swim. Salt water is particularly buoyant, the atmosphere can be more relaxed than in the confined, sometimes crowded space of a pool and there is often a large area of very shallow water. (See page 24 for the shallow water method of learning to swim.)

Some young children are very frightened of the sea and need the same sort of handling as timid children at the pool. Never force them into the sea. Just let them play on the beach, encouraging them gradually to get nearer to the water's edge.

Children often learn to swim in shallow sea-water.

Water temperature

Children get cold quicker than adults because they have less body fat and they should not stay in the sea when they are cold. It is not a good idea to put babies in any but the very warmest sea because they have no shiver reflex and can get dangerously cold with no apparent symptoms. Toddlers and young children also need to be watched very carefully.

If your child is shivering, get him out and wrap him in towels but don't rub him down. It is most important to keep the body's internal organs warm and rubbing only takes the blood away from these to bring it to the body surface.

Wrap a cold child in towels but don't rub him down.

Safety

It is vitally important to take special care about safety in the sea. Follow the precautions listed on the right and instill them into your child. Some of the pool precautions also apply to the sea (see page 13).

◄ Never swim where a warning, for example a red flag, is displayed.

◄ Don't swim in places where you have no information about the state of tides and currents.

◄ Never swim unless a competent adult is watching all the time. Young children should have an adult in the water with them.

◄ Only go out a short way, then swim parallel to the shore. This is especially important if the tide is going out, as it will be harder to swim back than it was to swim out.

◄ It is safest not to play on air-beds or in inflatable toy boats. Tides, winds and currents can quickly take you out to sea.

◄ Don't swim near boats, windsurfers or surfers.

51

* The sea is unlikely ever to be warm enough for babies.

DIVING

Diving can add a completely new dimension to a swimming session and provide children with a lot of enjoyment and a sense of achievement. Some children take to diving much more naturally than others, however, and there is no point in forcing a child who does not enjoy it.

Before your child starts diving, she needs to be thoroughly confident about swimming in deep water, jumping into deep water and swimming underwater with her eyes open. She also needs to have good breath control. Before she starts diving proper, she should try the preliminary practices described on these two pages. The submerging, stretching and jumping practices can all be done in the shallow end.

Always make sure that the water is deep enough for diving. It needs to be at least 2m (6ft 6in) for children attempting the dives described on pages 54-55.

Instill into children that their hands must always enter the water first when they dive and that they should keep their heads firmly between their arms to avoid any risk of head or spine injuries.

Submerging practices

- Blow bubbles in the water (see page 22).

- Go down to touch the pool floor.

- Count how many fingers someone is holding up under the water.

- Swim through someone's legs.

Stretching practices

Keep your head in line with your body and your arms against your ears for these practices.

- Standing on the poolside, stretch up as tall as possible.

- Push and glide from the side on front and back (see page 21).

- Push and glide from the side, then roll from front to back and vice versa.

- Push and glide from the side into a forward or backward somersault.

- Do a mushroom float (see page 45), then stretch out horizontally.

- Push and glide from the side to the pool bottom, then surface, either by turning your fingers up or pushing off with your feet.

- Do several surface dives (see page 48) one after the other like a porpoise.

- Do a handstand, concentrating on getting a good stretch.

Practices for getting into the water

- Jump in from the side, forwards and backwards, making different shapes in the air. (See page 47 for different types of jump and how to surface.)

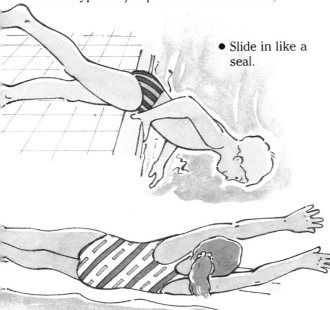

- Slide in like a seal.

- Roll in sideways like a log.

- Crouch on the edge in a tight ball, head tucked in, arms round your legs, and roll in forwards. Don't lift your head.

Jumping practices

- Jump as high as possible out of the water, keeping your body streamlined and stretched.

- Jump as high as possible and make different shapes in the air.

- Jump as high as possible and turn in the air, keeping your body stream-lined and stretched.

- Jump and dive over a partner's arms, held on the surface of the water.

- Jump into a handstand. 53

Sitting dive

You may prefer to dive in from a sitting position to begin with.

Sit down with your feet on the rail or trough. Then raise your arms above your head and, keeping them against your ears, put your head down to your chest.

Taking care to keep your arms and head in this position, bend forward until you overbalance, then push off from the rail and stretch forward and down.

Kneeling dive

You may like to start diving from a position with one foot in front of the other. In this case make sure that your front foot grips the edge of the pool very firmly to

avoid slipping and progress to a two-footed take-off as soon as possible so your dives do not run the risk of becoming lop-sided.

Go down on one knee at the edge of the pool with the toes of your front foot gripping the edge, the toes of your back foot curled under. Your arms and head are positioned as for the sitting dive.

Lean forward until you overbalance, then push off with the front foot and stretch forward and down, taking special care to keep your head down because of the greater height involved.

Crouch dive

Crouch on the poolside, with your toes gripping the edge and your arms and head in the same position as before.

This time, as you overbalance and push off, try to get your legs straighter and aim for a less flat entry into the water.

Lunge dive

This is a progression from a kneeling dive.

Your front leg should be well bent as you stand on the edge, your back leg straighter. Remember to grip the edge firmly with your toes. Arms and head should be in the same position as before.

As you overbalance and push off with your front leg, lift your back leg into the air, then bring both legs together during flight. Aim to enter the water well away from the side.

Plunge dive

This is a progression from a crouch dive and forms the basis for racing dives.

Crouch on the edge as shown above, eyes looking at the point where you aim to enter the water.

As you overbalance forwards, swing your arms into position, lower your head and push off vigorously with your feet.

Stretch as fully as possible during flight and aim to enter the water at an angle of between 15° and 20°. Keep the streamlined position until you are completely submerged. To surface, tilt your fingers upwards and raise your head. Glide as far as possible before starting to swim.

GAMES

Playing games in the water not only provides relaxation and enjoyment but can also encourage children to be more versatile.

The type of games you can play in a public pool will depend on its rules and regulations and on how crowded it is. The games on the right do not include those which require balls or other equipment as most pools do not allow these except in organized classes. In the sea, balls can be dangerous as they tend to float or blow out to sea and children are tempted to follow them.

You will need to supervise all games especially closely; accidents are more likely to happen if children are excited and playing in a group. Children who are not totally competent when out of their depth should wear armbands.

The games described here will give you a few ideas for what you can do. Most of them will probably work best with more than the minimum number of players. You may be able to adapt the games, or invent others, to suit the age, ability level and number of children involved. Don't forget the value of action songs and rhymes especially for younger children (see page 17).

On-the-spot games

Electricity
(3 or more players)
Stand in a circle holding hands. One player "switches on" the current by squeezing the hand of the person next to her. This player squeezes the hand of the person next to her and then ducks under the water. This continues round the circle.

Still pond
(3 or more players)
Everyone floats as still as possible while one person watches. The last one to move is the winner.

Kick-of-war
(2 or more players)
Hold a float between you while lying on your front, then kick to push each other backwards.

If there are four or more players, divide into two teams, each player lightly holding the ankles of the person in front and the two front members of each team holding the float. All kick to push the opposing team backwards.

Chasing games

Sharks and minnows
(3 or more players)
One person is the shark and stands in the middle of the pool. The others are minnows and line up at one side. When the shark shouts "sharks and minnows", they have to try and reach the other side without being caught. As soon as someone is caught, they change into a shark and help to catch the remaining minnows. Last one to be caught becomes the shark next game.

Crows and cranes
(3 or more players)
The players line up on each side of the pool. One person stands in the middle with a float. She calls out the names of two people, one from each side, and they have to race to the middle, take the float and try to get it back to their side without their opposite number touching them. If a player is touched, he gets a penalty point or becomes the person with the float.

Races

Skill races
(2 or more players)
Besides ordinary swimming races and
relay races, try races where you have to
run, jump, hop, side-step, run backwards
or walk on your hands.

Bubble-blowing race
(2 or more players)
Walk or run, stopping to put your face in
the water and blow bubbles every time
you have gone an agreed number of
paces.

Tunnel swim
(2 or more pairs)
Split into two teams. Each team stands in
line, one player in front of the other, legs
apart. The person at the back of each
team swims through the team's legs and
stands up at the front. The next person
then sets off and so on, until all the team
has swum through.

Wheelbarrow race
(2 or more pairs)
One partner supports the other's legs and
pushes him forwards. The "wheelbarrow"
can either swim with his arms or keep
them outstretched.

Pair swim
(2 or more pairs)
Each pair links arms, then pushes off from
the side and swims an agreed distance
together.

Shadow swim
(2 or more pairs)
One partner swims underwater, while the
other shadows him at the surface.

Chain swim
(2 or more pairs)
Divide into two teams and swim joined up,
lightly holding the ankles of the person in
front.

Statues
(4 or more players)
You have to stand still when "it" catches
you or touches a certain part of your body
(agreed beforehand). You can only be
"unfrozen" by another player touching
you or swimming through your legs. Last
one to be caught becomes "it".

What time is it, Mr Shark?
(3 or more players)
The shark stands at one side of the pool,
hands over his eyes, back to the other
players, who line up on the other side.
They shout "What time is it, Mr Shark?";
he replies, for example: "5 o'clock", and
they can then take five paces forwards.
The aim is to reach and touch the other
side but when the shark thinks they are
getting close he suddenly shouts "dinner
time", turns round and chases them. If he
catches someone before they get back to
their own side, they become Mr Shark.

Log roll tag
(3 or more players)
"It" sculls or floats on his back while the
others move round him in a circle, trying
to get as close as possible. He suddenly
rolls over and tries to catch someone.
When someone is caught, they become
"it".

Red letter
(3 or more players)
"It" stands at one side of the pool, hands
over his eyes, back to the other players,
who line up on the other side. "It" calls
out letters of the alphabet; whenever he
calls a letter that is in a player's name,
that player can take a step forward. The
aim is to reach and touch the other side
but when they are getting close "it"
suddenly shouts "red letter", turns round
and chases them. If someone is caught
before they get back to their own side,
they become "it".

57

COPING WITH EMERGENCIES

Teaching your child to swim is the best possible safety measure you can take to protect her when she is in or near water. Remember that the survival skills described on pages 44-49 are as important as the swimming strokes.

Special precautions which need to be taken at swimming pools are described on page 13 and in the sea on page 51. In this section are a few more things to remember and to instill into your child in case she is ever in difficulty, as well as some rudimentary advice on how to help others in trouble. You are most likely to help others successfully, without putting yourself in unnecessary danger, if you have followed a proper life-saving course. These are available for competent swimmers of all ages.*

What to do if you are in trouble

Try to keep calm. If you are near the edge of the water, try to reach it and get out. If you cannot, see if there is anything you can hold on to while you shout for help and wave one arm to attract attention.

If you fall into water with your clothes on, take off anything heavy like a coat or shoes which will drag you down. Light clothes help to retain body heat, so you should leave those on.

Try to keep afloat with the minimum of exertion. The survival skills which will help you do this are described on pages 44-46. Treading water can be especially useful because you can wave one arm as you do it to attract attention, as shown on the left. Exerting yourself as little as possible is important not only to prevent you getting tired but also to help keep you warm if you are in cold water, that is water of less than 25°C (77°F).** Any movement will lead to a drop in body temperature by increasing the blood flow to the body surface; this blood is cooled by the water and then circulates round the body, lowering its temperature.

What to do if someone else is in trouble

Shout for help or send someone to fetch help. Don't get in the water yourself if you can possibly rescue the person without doing so. He may be panicking and drag you down with him. Speak to him calmly and keep any instructions clear and simple.

Casualty near the edge

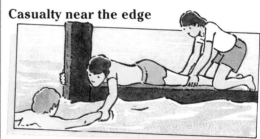

If the person is near the edge of the water, lie down flat and try to grab his wrist (don't let him grab you), holding on to something secure if possible. Getting down low and grabbing the wrist rather than the hand reduces the risk of being dragged in yourself. If anyone else is with you, they should kneel down and hold your legs.

If the person is too far out to reach with your hand, quickly look for something to extend your reach: a stick or branch, rope, scarf, towels or clothes, knotted together if necessary. Lie down as you haul the person in.

*Ask for more information at your local pool, library or council.
**In Britain the sea temperature seldom reaches 15°C (59°F).

Casualty further out

If the person is too far out to reach, throw something that will float, such as a beach ball, rubber ring, or plank of wood, for him to hold on to. Don't aim it directly at him but try to make sure it lands within easy reach. Once he is holding the object, tell him either to stay where he is or to try to reach safety by kicking his legs.

Casualty quite far out in shallow water

If there are other people around, you may be able to make a human chain. The person nearest the edge holds on to something secure, while the others grasp wrists, facing in opposite directions, until someone can reach the casualty with a stick or some clothing, or throw him something that floats.

If you are alone, you may be able to wade in until you are close enough to throw him something or hold something out to him. If you hold something out, first lean backwards and get a firm foothold to avoid being pulled over.

Casualty quite far out in deep water

Sculling

Upside-down breast stroke

If you are a very good swimmer, you could swim out to the rescue with a floating object. Take off any bulky clothes and your shoes first. Be sure to push the object towards her so that she grabs it rather than you. Now you can wait with her until help arrives, go back on your own to fetch help or encourage her to swim back with you, as she holds on to the object and kicks her legs.

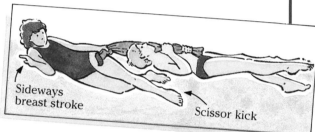

Sideways breast stroke

Scissor kick

As a last resort it may be possible to give the casualty some clothing to hang on to so that you can tow him in, swimming a form of side stroke or on your back.

How to get the casualty out of the water

If the person cannot get out of the water on his own, tell him to hold on to something and get out yourself. Then, holding his wrists and bending your knees, lift him up and down two or three times to make him more buoyant. Be careful not to submerge his face. Now lift him up over the edge, letting him rest first of all on your extended straight leg, before you lower his body gently to the ground. Take care to protect his head as you do this. Now lift his legs over the edge.

Rest his body on your leg.

Resuscitation

If a person is unconscious, it is possible that they are not breathing. Their heart may also have stopped beating. In either case, it is vital that resuscitation be started immediately. You need to get oxygen into their lungs and get their heart to pump the oxygenated blood round their body. The brain suffers particularly quickly from lack of oxygen.

Never practice this on a healthy person.

Artificial respiration

Check for signs of consciousness by gently shaking and shouting at the casualty. If you cannot see, hear or feel him breathing, send for medical help immediately and prepare to start artificial respiration.

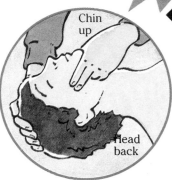

Chin up

Head back

First clear his mouth of any obstruction, such as seaweed or vomit. Then tilt his head back with his chin lifted up. This straightens out the airways and removes the tongue from the back of the throat, and he may start breathing again spontaneously. If so, put him in the recovery position (see page 62). If he is breathing only faintly, or not at all, start artificial respiration.

Mouth to mouth and nose

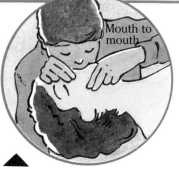

Mouth to mouth

If the casualty is a baby or child, keep his head tilted back, open his mouth, then seal your lips around his mouth and nose, and breathe into his lungs four times gently and fairly quickly. (Blow from your cheeks rather than breathing deeply from your lungs.)

If the casualty is an adult, keep his head tilted back, open his mouth with one hand and with your other hand pinch his nostrils firmly together. Then seal your lips around his mouth and breathe into his lungs four times deeply and fairly quickly so that you fill them with air.

Watch for chest movement. If he does not start breathing, check to see if his heart is beating. (See top of page opposite.) If it is not, start external chest compression. If the heart is beating, just continue with artificial respiration until he starts breathing. Give one breath at five second intervals.

Artificial respiration in the water

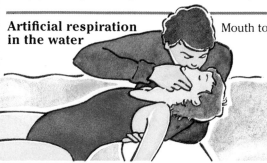

Mouth to nose

It may be necessary to start artificial respiration while you are still in the water. If you are within your depth, try to support the casualty's body with one arm, hold her chin firmly with the other hand, closing her mouth, and blow into her nose.

60

External chest compression

If artificial respiration alone does not get the person breathing and her heart has stopped, you will need to perform external chest compression in conjunction with artificial respiration.

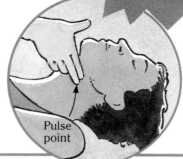

Pulse point

Never try external chest compression if the heart is beating, however faintly.

◀ Check whether her heart is beating by taking the pulse in her neck. You should be able to find this just below the jaw bone in the hollow between the voice box and the adjoining muscle.

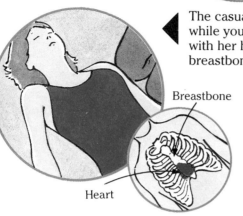

Breastbone

Heart

◀ The casualty should lie on her back on a firm surface while you kneel alongside, facing her chest and in line with her heart. Pressure needs to be applied to the breastbone. (See "Rates of chest compression" below.)

Follow every 15 compressions by two breaths of artificial respiration. Check to see whether the heart is beating after the first minute and then every three minutes.

When the heartbeat returns, stop compressions immediately and continue with artificial respiration alone until she is breathing naturally. Then put her in the recovery position (see page 62).

Rates of chest compression

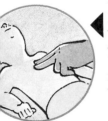

◀ For babies and young children use very gentle pressure with two fingers only. Press on the center of the breastbone at a rate of 100 times per minute to a depth of 1.5 to 2.5cm (0.5 to 1in).

◀ For children use light pressure with the heel of one hand only. Press on the center of the breastbone at a rate of 100 times per minute to a depth of 2.5 to 3.5cm (1 to 1.5in).

◀ For older children and adults, use the heel of one hand, covered with the heel of the other, fingers locked together. Keep your arms straight and rock forward until they are vertical. Press at a rate of 80 times per minute to a depth of 4 to 5cm (1.5 to 2in). Rock backwards to release pressure.

Remember

- Send for medical help right away.
- It is vital to get the person breathing. Don't waste time dealing with small injuries.
- People often vomit before they lapse into, or as they come round from, unconsciousness. Roll him on to his side if this happens so he does not choke.
- An unconscious person cannot be woken, does not respond to pinching and has dilated pupils.
- Never leave an unconscious person alone. He may stop breathing and need resuscitation.
- It can take a long time to resuscitate someone. Don't give up until help arrives.

The recovery position

This is the best position for an unconscious person who is breathing and whose heart is beating to lie in. The airways are clear so she can breathe easily and will not choke.

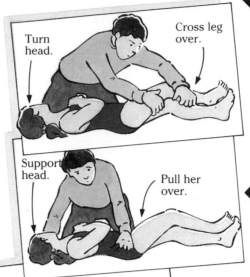

Turn head.

Cross leg over.

Support head.

Pull her over.

▶ To put her in the recovery position, turn her head towards you, place the arm nearest you palm down underneath her body, cross her other arm over her chest and bend the leg furthest from you over the other one.

▶ Support her head with your hand and roll her over by pulling on her swimsuit or clothes around the hips.

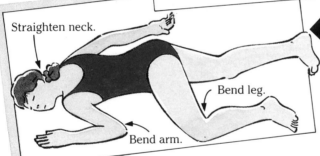

Straighten neck.

Bend leg.

Bend arm.

▶ Bend her top leg up towards her chest, ease her lower arm away from her body and keep the airways open by tipping her chin upwards to straighten her neck. Don't put anything under her head. Help to keep her warm by putting something over her and, preferably, under her as well.

GOING FURTHER

Beginners' swimming classes are an excellent way to help children become confident in the water. There are classes too for swimmers who want to learn more advanced strokes and skills and there are also clubs for children of different ages and levels of ability.

Besides improving children's general swimming and allowing them to meet other swimmers, classes and clubs help them to develop or follow up an interest in a particular aspect of swimming – perhaps learning life-saving, entering competitions or getting involved in synchronized swimming

(water ballet). They will also provide information about the many nationally recognized awards which children can take at different levels and in different types of swimming.

The best place to find out about classes and clubs in your area is from the notice board at your local swimming pool. The local council (recreation and amenities department) should also have lists and your local library may have information. Remember always to make sure that any class or club is run by people with a recognized qualification.*

* In America this will be from the American Red Cross, American Alliance for Health, Physical Education, Recreation and Dance (AAHPERD) and YMCA.

WORDS OF SONGS

Below are the words of the action songs suggested on pages 16, 17 and 24.

General songs (see page 17)

If you're happy and you know it,
Splash your hands;
If you're happy and you know it,
Splash your hands;
If you're happy and you know it,
And you really want to show it;
If you're happy and you know it,
Splash your hands.

Ring-a-ring o' roses,
A pocket full of posies,
A-tishoo, a-tishoo!
We all blow bubbles.

Here we go round the mulberry bush,
The mulberry bush, the mulberry bush,
Here we go round the mulberry bush
On a cold and frosty morning.

(Walk round in a circle.)

This is the way we jump up and down,
Jump up and down, jump up and down,
This is the way we jump up and down,
On a cold and frosty morning.

All the above songs can be repeated with different verses and actions, as appropriate, for example: kick your legs, turn around, wash your face, have a shower, wash your hair.

Oh, the Grand Old Duke of York,
He had ten thousand men,
(Walk on the spot.)
He marched them up to the top of the hill,
(Walk forwards.)
And he marched them down again.
(Walk backwards.)
And when they were up, they were up,
(Walk forwards.)
And when they were down, they were down,
(Walk backwards.)
And when they were only half way up,
(One step forwards.)
They were neither up nor down.
(One step backwards.)

Try also playing "Simon says". Simon shouts instructions such as "Simon says, 'put your hands in the air'," and everyone has to obey unless he leaves out "Simon says", when they must not. Don't make anyone who makes a mistake be "out" though.

Bouncing songs (see page 16)

Up and down the City Road,
In and out of the Eagle,
That's the way the money goes,
Pop goes the weasel!

Half a pound of tuppenny rice,
Half a pound of treacle,
Mix it up and make it nice,
Pop goes the weasel!

Every night when I go out,
The monkey's on the table,
Take a stick and knock it off,
Pop goes the weasel!

One potato, two potato,
Three potato, four;
Five potato, six potato,
Seven potato, more!

Trickling water songs (see page 17)

It's raining, it's pouring,
The old man is snoring;
He got into bed and bumped his head,
And couldn't get up in the morning.

Doctor Foster went to Gloucester
In a shower of rain;
He stepped in a puddle,
Right up to his middle,
And never went there again.

Rolling over song (see page 24)

There were ten in the bed,
And the little one said,
"Roll over, roll over";
So they all rolled over,
And one fell out,
There were nine in the bed,
And the little one said,
"Roll over, roll over"; . . .

(Continue down to one.)

INDEX

First published in 1988 by Usborne Publishing Ltd, 20 Garrick Street, London WC2 9BJ, England.
Copyright © Usborne Publishing Ltd 1988.
The name Usborne and the device ♈ are Trade Marks of Usborne Publishing Ltd.
American edition 1989.